The Joy of Mozart

Selected and edited by Denes Agay.

For over two centuries the works of Mozart have provided mankind with abundant musical pleasures. The appeal of this master's music has been universal and constant, unaffected by geographic boundaries and stylistic changes. The "genius of light and love" - as Wagner referred to him - composed his first minuet at the age of five and created during a brief lifespan of 35 years a unique catalogue of masterpieces in all media of musical expression. This great body of music, in terms of exquisite melody, simplicity of structure and perfect balance of form and content, has seldom been paralled and never surpassed.

The Joy of Mozart represents a sampler of this musical treasury. The first section contains a graded repertory of his keyboard works from the charming miniatures of early childhood to the masterly, almost Chopinesque, Rondo in A minor (K511). The second section consists of selected, favorite themes and excerpts from the piano concertos, operas, and various orchestral works, arranged for piano solo in the easy-to-intermediate range. The volume concludes with a digest of themes from the lovely Serenade *Eine kleine Nachtmusik*, a popular opus which, we believe is rarely encountered in solo piano version.

We trust this collection will gratify all those who seek the finest in music for both education and diversion. To paraphrase Keats: the music of Mozart, an unquestionable thing of beauty, is a joy forever.

Order Number: YK 30021
US International Standard Book Number: 0.8256.8025.5
UK International Standard Book Number: 0.7119.0331.X

Exclusive Distributors:
Music Sales Corporation
257 Park Avenue South, New York, New York 10010 USA
Music Sales Limited
8/9 Frith Street, London W1V 5TZ England
Music Sales Pty. Limited
120 Rothschild Street, Rosebery, Sydney, NSW 2018, Australia

Printed in the United States of America by
Vicks Lithograph and Printing Corporation

Yorktown Music Press
London/New York/Sydney

CONTENTS

Keyboard Works:

Favorite Themes from Piano Concertos, Operas and Orchestral Works:
Arranged by Denes Agay

Menuet

K.7

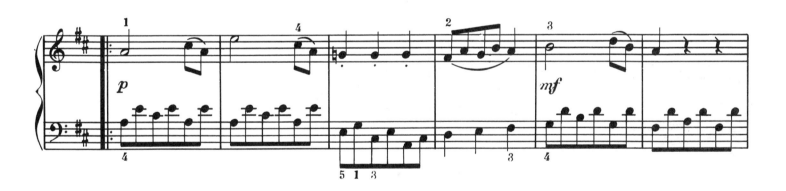

Allegro

K.3g

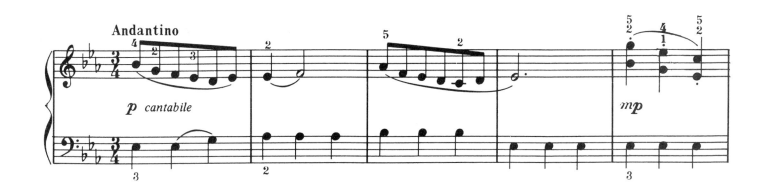

Air

K.16kk

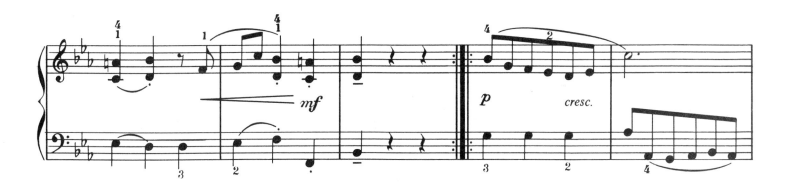

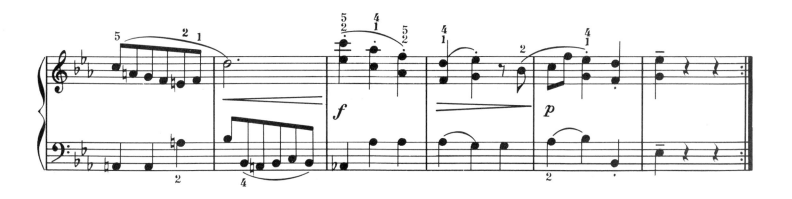

Menuetto

K.15qq

Andante

K.15mm

Spring Song

K.596

Original piano part of the song,"Come,Sweet May."

Contredance in A

K.151

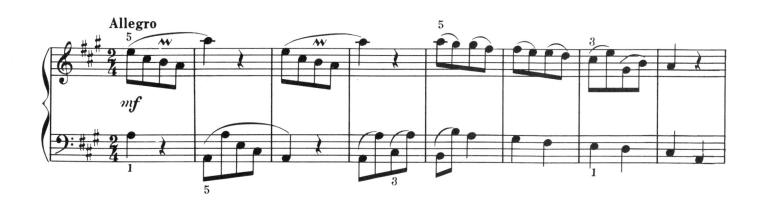

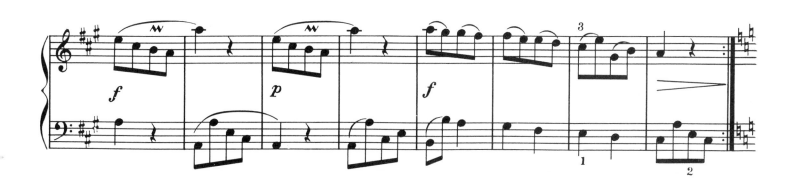

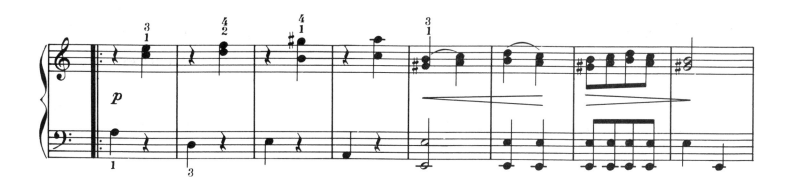

Minuet and Trio

K.315a

Trio

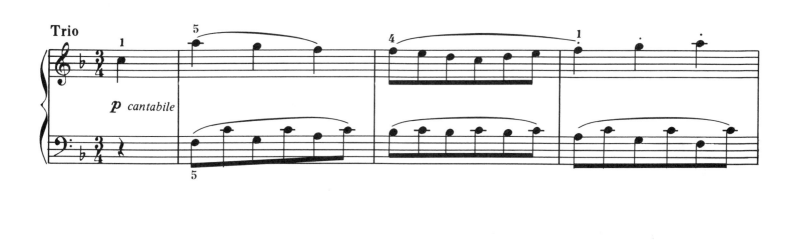

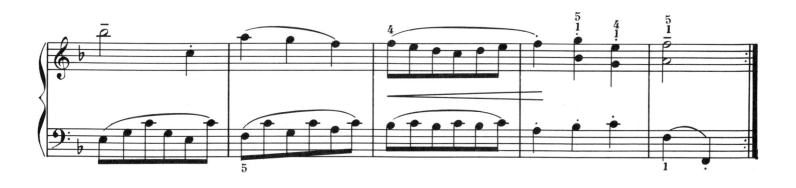

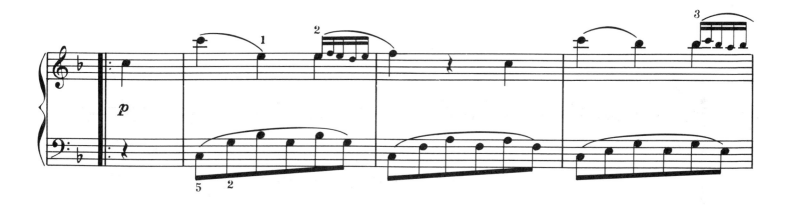

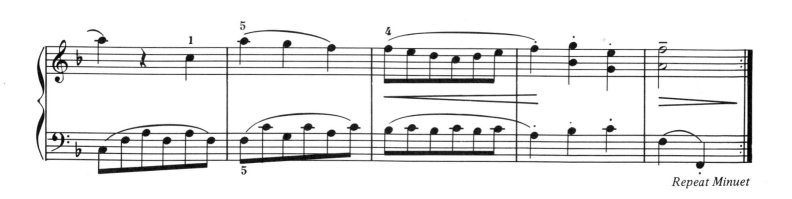

Repeat Minuet

Burleska

Composed in 1766

Rondino
K.15d

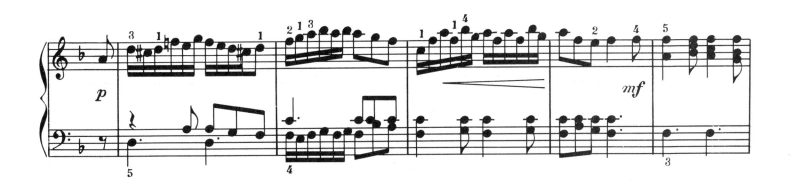

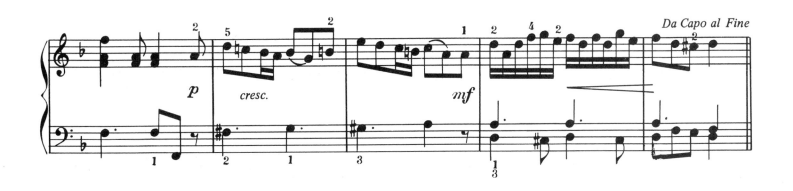

Sonatina

I

Coda

II Rondo

Andante Cantabile

from Sonata in C - K.330

Rondo

K.15hh

*Small notes are editorial additions and may be omitted.

Alla Turca

from Sonata K.331

Viennese Sonatina No. 2

MENUETTO
Allegretto

Variations on an Allegretto
K.54

36

VAR.3

VAR.4

* Original dynamic marks.

Sonata

K.-Anh.135-547a

Allegretto

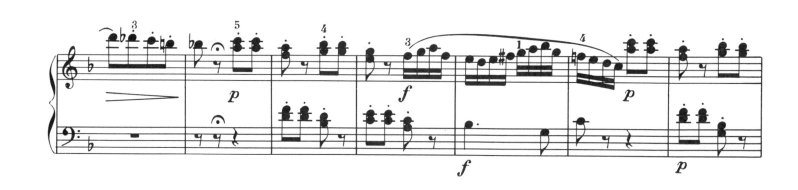

Rondo

K.511

53

Theme from "The Marriage of Figaro"

Non più andrai

Themes from "The Magic Flute"

(Dies Bildneis)
Larghetto

Theme from "Don Giovanni"

La ci darem la mano

Theme from Piano Concerto No. 24

C minor K.491-Second Movement

Theme from Piano Conerto No. 21

K.467-Second Movement

Theme from Piano Concerto No. 15

Bb Major K.450-Third Movement

Theme from Piano Concerto No. 17

G Major K.453-Third Movement

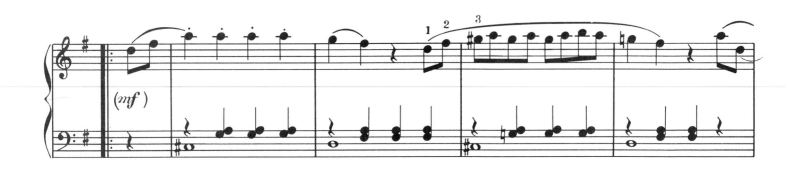

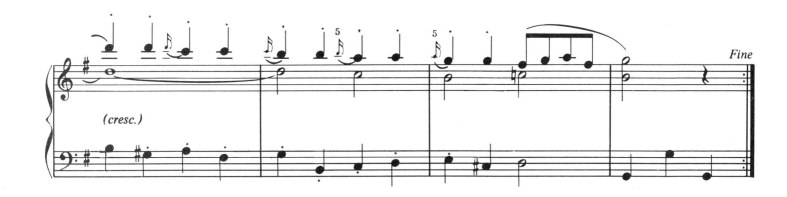

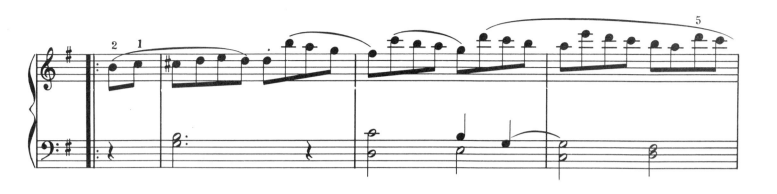

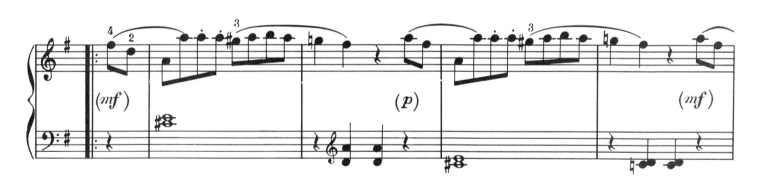

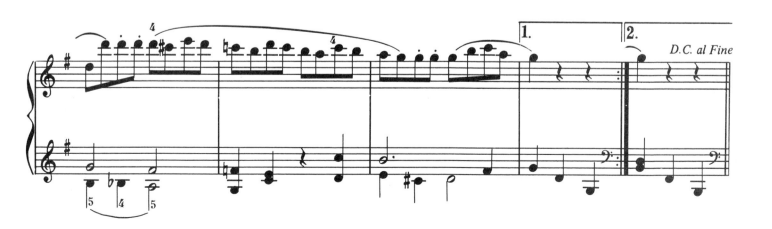

Theme from Symphony No. 40

G minor-K.550

A Little Night Music

Eine Kleine Nachtmusik

I

* *Transcribed for Piano Solo by Denes Agay*

II

(Romanza)
Andante

Fine

III

(Menuetto)
Allegretto

IV